'Know the Game' Series
GOLF

CONTENTS

FOREWORD

The origins of the game of golf have been the subject of much research for many years and still arouse controversy.

It is considered that the game began in Scotland, although several landscapes painted by Dutch and Flemish artists suggest that golf was played in Holland before it was known in Scotland.

The first mention of the game in official records was during the Scottish Parliaments of 1457–1491 when golf was prohibited due to its popularity interfering with the practice of archery, to the consequent detriment of the national defence in the wars against England; by the reign of James II golf had become a national pastime in Scotland.

The Honourable Company of Edinburgh Golfers situated at Muirfield formed the first set of Rules of the game, and these were adopted by the Society of St. Andrews Golfers which was formed in 1754.

In 1834 King William IV approved the change of name of the Society to the Royal and Ancient Golf Club of St. Andrews, which is responsible for the government of the game, the interpretation of the Rules and the control of the Open Championship.

The following organisations are responsible for the control of amateur golf in their respective areas: The English Golf Union (founded 1924), The Golfing Union of Ireland (founded 1891), The Scottish Golf Union (founded 1920) and the Welsh Golfing Union (founded 1895).

With the spread of the game overseas many organisations have been formed, the most significant being the United States Golf Association founded in 1894, which is responsible for governing all aspects of the game in America and has close contact with the Royal and Ancient Golf Club to maintain uniformity in the administration of the game.

In 1927 Mr. Samuel Ryder presented the Ryder Cup for competition between professionals from America and Britain, and the contest takes place in alternate years, each country being visited in turn.

The Professional Golfers' Association was founded in 1901 to promote interest in the game of golf and to protect and advance the mutual and trade interests of its members. The P.G.A. is the oldest such Association in the world and is responsible for promoting professional tournaments run under its auspices in the British Isles.

It is most advantageous for any beginner to the game to seek advice from any golf professional who is a member of the P.G.A. He will advise on correct equipment and give tuition on the basic fundamentals of the game which are described in this book; the book is essentially a guide to the game and is not meant to be a complete reference.

If you have any doubt or query do not hesitate to ask your professional or Golf Club secretary for information; he will be only too pleased to give assistance. Irrespective of the degree of playing ability actually attained, golf is a pastime which can be enjoyed by young and old alike, and I have pleasure in recommending this book to all who wish to know the game of golf.

Colin Snape
Secretary, Professional Golfers' Association.

THE GAME

Rule 1 states:

"The Game of Golf consists in playing a ball from the teeing ground into the hole by successive strokes in accordance with the Rules."

A full-sized course consists of 18 holes, with usually four "short" holes, which measure up to 250 yards from tee to green and can be covered by one full stroke, and 14 longer holes, from 220 to 500 yards or more in length, and requiring two or three full strokes from tee to green. One round of the course is the usual length of a match, but in some competitions two or more rounds are played. One round occupies about three hours.

The space between tee and green at the long holes is occupied by mown turf called the "fairway" and on either side of the fairway are rough grass, trees, bushes, etc. There are also "hazards" of various kinds, mainly sand bunkers but occasionally streams, ditches, and ponds. The green is a closely mown surface for putting and the "hole" is usually sunk in the middle of the green.

ETIQUETTE

In addition to the rules, the game also has a code of etiquette, which should be observed by all golfers and studied with particular care by beginners. Adherence to these rules of behaviour helps to make the game more enjoyable for everyone. The rules are quoted in full on page 35, but can be summarised as follows:

Do not move, talk, stand close to or directly behind the ball or the hole when a player is making a stroke.

Do not play until the match in front is out of range, but do not unnecessarily delay play.

If overtaken by a following match while searching for a ball, or because of your own slow play, signal to the overtaking players to pass, and then wait until they have gone out of range before continuing play.

Smooth over holes and footmarks made in bunker sand before leaving it, and see that all turf cut by the club-head is replaced and pressed down.

Avoid damage to greens by clubs, feet or flagstick, and repair marks made by the ball when landing. After replacing flagstick walk off quickly when the result of the hole is determined, without re-trying putts, so that the way is clear for following players.

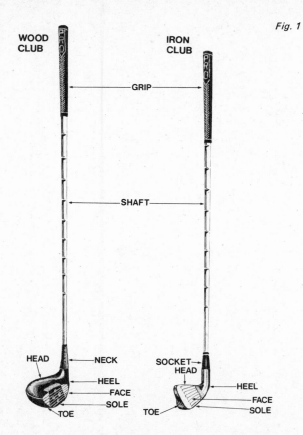

WOOD
CLUB

IRON
CLUB

GRIP

SHAFT

HEAD — NECK
HEEL
FACE
SOLE
TOE

SOCKET
HEAD
TOE
HEEL
FACE
SOLE

Fig. 1

THE CLUB AND THE BALL

Rule 2 prohibits the use of any club or ball which does not conform to clearly-defined specifications and fundamental principles of design. Clubs must have all the various parts fixed and not capable of adjustment. Concave faces are banned, also those having markings which do not satisfy requirements or are modified for the purpose of unduly influencing the movement of the ball.

The grip on the shaft may not have a channel or furrow or be moulded to the hands, and the shaft itself must be fixed to the heel of the club-head, except in the case of a putter. The shaft of a putter may be fixed at any point in the head but must be straight and must diverge from the vertical by at least ten degrees from a point not more than five inches above the sole.

An "iron" club is one with a head which is usually relatively narrow from face to back, and is usually made of steel. A "wood" club is one with a head relatively broad from face to back, and is usually made of wood, plastic, or a light metal. A modern phenomenon of club manufacture is the use of the carbon fibre or "graphite" shaft.

The weight of the ball shall be not greater than 1·62 ounces (45·9 grammes) and the size not less than 1·62 inches (41·2 mm) in diameter. The minimum diameter in the United States and some other countries is 1·68 inches (42·7 mm) and since 1968 this larger ball has been in use in all tournaments run under the auspices of the PGA.

Fig. 2

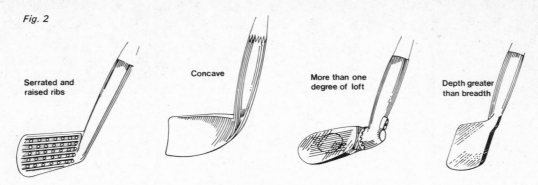

Serrated and raised ribs

Concave

More than one degree of loft

Depth greater than breadth

Some old-fashioned club heads now illegal

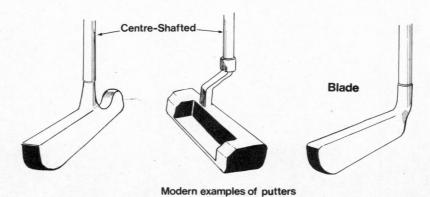

Centre-Shafted

Blade

Modern examples of putters

Fig. 3

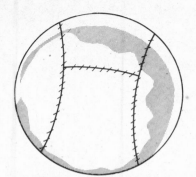

Fig. 4

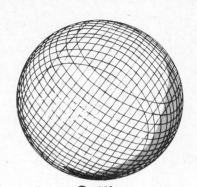

**Old-fashioned ball stuffed
with feathers**

Guttie

Rubber Core

Discussions started in 1970 with the object of reaching a compromise between the British and American sizes and so achieving uniformity throughout the world. The 1·66 inch ball (42·2 mm) is a possibility of the future.

Although golf in its earliest and unrecorded days was probably played with odd missiles such as pebbles or lumps of wood, the first ball known to history was the "featherie"—a leather bag stuffed tightly with feathers and then stitched. This was at best an ill-flying ball with a very short life, particularly in wet weather, but it remained in general use for more than two centuries until the advent of the "guttie" about 120 years ago. This was made from gutta-percha, softened and cast in a spherical mould, originally hand-hammered to make it fly straight. Later, moulds with embossed or recessed patterns came into use.

In the late 1890s the Haskell ball, made from strip rubber wound round a core, was produced in America, and first used in Britain in 1902. It soon ousted the guttie, and the rubber-core ball, as it is called, is now made to perfection by up-to-date machinery and with reasonable care will last for many rounds of golf without losing shape or resilience.

STANCE

Definition 1: A player has "addressed the ball" when he has taken his stance and has also grounded his club (or, in a hazard, has taken his stance).

The stance, or position taken by the feet in preparing for the stroke, varies with the build of the player, his method of swinging, and the type of shot being attempted, but, generally speaking, the feet are straddled along a line which is parallel to the line of intended flight.

The width of the stance also varies with players and types of shot, but a good rule is to stand so that the distance between the feet about equals the width of the shoulders. As the shots to the green get shorter so the stance narrows. The whole idea should be minimum width of stance consistent with balance. Too wide a stance restricts the pivoting of the body. Too narrow a stance makes the body sway, which is fatal.

There are three basic stances: Square, Open and Closed; and the one used depends upon the club chosen and the type of shot to be played.

THE SQUARE STANCE is used for most long shots with the woods and long irons.

THE OPEN STANCE mostly for bad lies, short shots, and approach play, etc.

THE CLOSED STANCE when it is necessary to put, draw or hook on the ball.

Open Stance

Fig. 5

Closed Stance

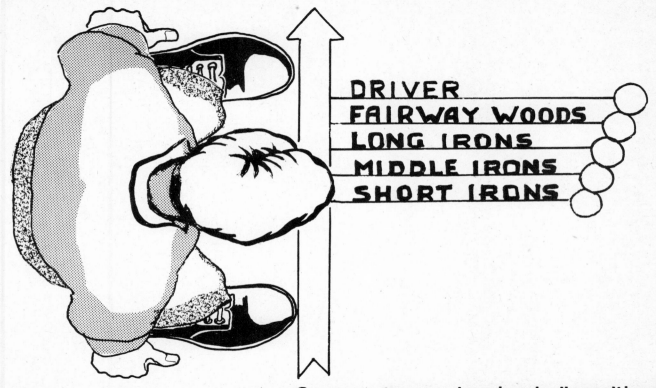

Fig. 6

Square stance, showing ball positions

DRIVER
FAIRWAY WOODS
LONG IRONS
MIDDLE IRONS
SHORT IRONS

ADDRESS

At the address position, the feet should be approximately as far apart as the width of the player's shoulders, with the weight evenly distributed between the feet: the toes should be pointed outwards very slightly and the knees flexed inwards. The left arm, wrist and club should be virtually in a straight line, with the hands slightly ahead of the club-head. The body should not be in a too crouched or an upright position, but just between the two.

BALL PLACEMENT

DRIVER: opposite the left heel.
FAIRWAY WOODS and
LONG IRONS: just inside the left heel.
MIDDLE IRONS: between the centre of the feet and the left heel, with the feet now getting closer together.
SHORT IRONS: midway between the feet which are now about nine inches apart.

The next thing to consider is the distance from the ball. This depends again on the build of the golfer and the size of club used, but the guiding factor is comfort and relaxation. One should feel comfortably settled down for hitting the ball, neither over-reaching for it nor hunched up. For the driver a good tip is to rest the club-head behind the ball and stand so that the outstretched left arm, holding the club, makes a straight line from shoulder to ball, while the body stands erect. Then bend forward to place the right hand on the shaft, and the position is correct. Another test is to take up a stance and then take away the right hand, dropping the club-head with the left until it touches the thigh just above the left knee. This shows again that the distance is correct.

THE GRIP

Although there are several ways of gripping a club, some of them highly unorthodox, the grip most commonly used is the overlapping or "Vardon" grip, so called after its originator Harry Vardon, who won the Open Championship on a record six occasions between 1896 and 1914.

Commence by placing the left hand on the club: it must be a combination of finger and palm grip. The club must lie across the hands from the middle joint of the first finger, over the base of the middle finger and into the heel of the hand. When the hand is closed, the thumb should be a quarter of the way round the shaft to the right and the tip of the thumb in line with the knuckle of the first finger. The "v" formed between the thumb and first finger should point between the chin and the right shoulder.

The right hand is a finger grip. To help the two hands to work together the little finger of the right hand overlaps the first finger of the left hand.

The grip lies across the middle joint of the other three fingers and the palm of the right hand fits snugly over the left thumb. The "v" formed between the thumb and forefinger also points to a spot between the chin and the right shoulder. There should now be a firm and lively connection of the hands and the club-head.

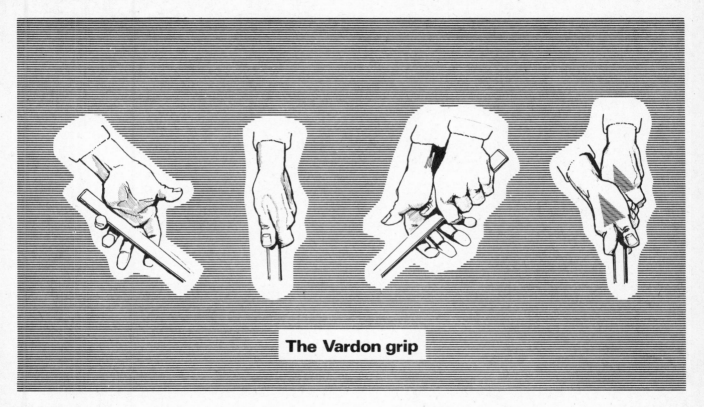

The Vardon grip

Fig. 7

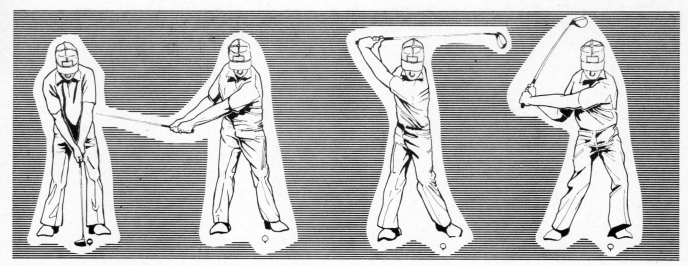

Fig. 8 (1)

MAKING THE STROKE

Definition 31 : A "stroke" is the forward movement of the club made with the intention of fairly striking at and moving the ball.

The mechanics of the golf swing consist in swinging the club backwards and upwards from the address position to a position above and behind the head from which a downward and forward blow can be aimed at the ball. The accompanying sketches should make clear the sequence of movements, but there are certain principles to bear in mind.

The club-head is taken back from the ball by a co-ordinated movement of various parts of the body, which pivots or turns on an axis formed by the spine. The hands lead while the left heel leaves the ground, the left knee bends inwards and sideways and the shoulders and hips turn. The head remains still throughout the swing, the chin pointing towards the ball, and when the club-head is half-way up to the top of the swing position the wrists begin to bend or "cock".

Fig. 8 (2)

At the top of the swing the club-shaft should be almost horizontal.

The start of the down-swing is a general "pull-down" of the left side, hands and arms leading, and then the rest of the down-swing is a progressive speeding up of the club-head, which is whipped into the ball in a flail-like manner. The whole movement, up and down, should be rhythmic and controlled.

A natural sequel to the down-swing is the "follow-through", in which the body turns in the direction of flight and the club-head is flung out in the same direction until at the finish of the stroke the trunk is square towards the hole, the hands high, and the club-shaft in a horizontal position behind the head.

The golf swing is more or less the same for all maximum-length shots, no matter what club is used, but in the case of short pitches or run-up shots when near to the green the back-swing must be restricted according to the length of the shot. This can only be judged by practice and experience.

13

RULES OF THE GAME

Rule 3

MAXIMUM OF 14 CLUBS

The player shall start a stipulated round with not more than 14 clubs. He may replace a club which becomes unfit for play but such replacement may not be made by borrowing from any other person playing on the course. (Penalty: Match Play: Loss of hole for each hole at which violation occurred with a maximum of two holes. Stroke Play: Two strokes for each hole at which violation occurred with a maximum of four strokes.)

A complete "matched set" of 14 clubs can be obtained, consisting usually of either four woods, nine irons and a putter or three woods, ten irons and a putter, depending on the individual preference of the player.

The length of a golf club varies from roughly 42 inches for a driver to 35 inches for a short iron or putter, diminishing at half-inch intervals. As the club diminishes in length, so the club face increases in weight and angle of loft; e.g. the driver at 42 inches has an angle of loft on its face of 11 degrees, the five iron at 38 inches has an angle of loft on its face of 30 degrees, and the wedge at 36 inches has an angle of 52 degrees. Women's clubs are lighter than those used by men, and matched sets are "fitted" to the players, some requiring lighter or shorter clubs than the standard sizes, or shafts with varying degrees of "whip".

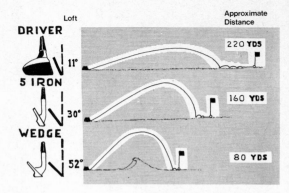

Fig. 9

Rule 4

AGREEMENT TO WAIVE RULES PROHIBITED

This rule states that players must not agree among themselves to waive a Rule or a Local Rule or any penalty incurred.

Rule 5

GENERAL PENALTY

Except when otherwise provided for, the penalty for a breach of a rule shall be the loss of a hole in match play or two strokes in stroke play.

Note: This is the usual penalty but certain minor infringements incur a penalty of one stroke. Generally speaking, disqualification occurs only in the case of deliberate infringement.

Rule 6

MATCH PLAY

In match play a hole is won by the side which holes its ball in the fewest strokes (after deducting any handicap allowance). The hole is halved if each side holes out in the same number of strokes. A match consists of a stipulated round or rounds, and is won by the side which is leading by a number of holes greater than the number remaining to be played.

Note: Thus, if a side is four up after playing 15 holes, they have won the match by four up and three to play (usually written as 4 & 3). If, after finishing the eighteenth hole, each side has won an equal number, the match is halved. If a decision is essential, as in a knock-out tournament or championship, it is usual for the players to begin the round again, the first to win a hole taking the match. Thus a game can be won at the 19th, the 20th and so on. In playing additional holes, handicap strokes are given and taken at the same holes as in the first round.

Rule 7

STROKE PLAY

The competitor who holes the stipulated round or rounds in the fewest strokes is the winner.

Note: In stroke competitions under handicap the full handicap allowed the player is deducted from his total, and the net score counts.

Rule 8

PRACTICE

During the play of a hole the player shall not play any practice stroke. Between the play of two holes a player shall not play a practice stroke from any hazard, or on to a putting green other than that of the hole last played. On any day of a stroke competition or play-off, the competitor shall not practise on the competition course before a round or play-off. When a competition extends over consecutive days, practice on the competition course between rounds is prohibited.

It is important to note that a practice swing is not a practice stroke, as a stroke is a forward movement of the club with the intention of striking the ball.

Rule 9

ADVICE AND ASSISTANCE

A player may give advice to, or ask advice from, only his partner or either of their caddies. In making a stroke a player shall not seek or accept physical assistance or protection from the elements. Except on the putting green (where only one's partner or caddie may do so) a player may have the line of play indicated by anyone; but no one shall place a mark or stand on the line of play while the stroke is being played.

Note: "Assistance" or "protection" would include such actions as bending back an obstructing bush or shielding the player from wind or rain.

Rule 10

INFORMATION AS TO STROKES TAKEN

A player who has incurred a penalty must tell his opponent or marker as soon as possible. The number of strokes a player has taken shall include any penalty strokes incurred. A player in match play is entitled at any time during the play of a hole to ascertain the number of strokes his opponent has taken. If the opponent gives wrong information and does not correct the mistake before the player has played his next stroke, the opponent shall lose the hole.

Rule 11

DISPUTES, DECISIONS AND DOUBTS AS TO RIGHTS

In match play where there is a dispute a claim must be made before the players strike off from the next teeing ground or (in the case of the last hole of the match) before they leave the putting green. Any later claim based on newly discovered facts cannot be considered unless the player making the claim had been given the wrong information by an opponent. In stroke play no penalty shall be imposed after a competition is closed unless wrong information had been given by the competitor. If a referee has been appointed by the Committee, his decision shall be final. In the absence of a referee, the decision of the Committee shall be final. If the Committee cannot come to a decision, it shall refer to the Rules of Golf Committee of the Royal and Ancient Golf Club of St. Andrews and their decision shall be final.

If any point in dispute be not covered by the Rules or Local Rules, the decision shall be made in accordance with equity.

In stroke play only a competitor doubtful of his rights or procedure may play out the hole with the ball in play and, at the same time, complete the play of the hole with a second ball stating which ball he wishes to score with if that procedure is allowable under the rules. The point is then referred to the committee for adjudication. If a player fails to state which ball he wants to count, the ball with higher score (if allowable under the rules) will count.

Rule 12

THE HONOUR

A match begins by each side playing a ball from the first teeing ground in order of the draw or by lot. The side which wins a hole takes "the honour", i.e. plays first, at the next teeing ground. In match play an opponent may recall a ball played out of turn, but in stroke play the stroke must stand. In neither case is there any penalty.

Definition 33: The teeing ground is the starting place for the hole to be played. It is a rectangular area two club-lengths in depth, the front and the sides of which are defined by the outside limits of two markers. A ball is outside the teeing ground when all of it lies outside the stipulated area.

Note: The teeing ground is not necessarily the whole of the flat space prepared for teeing, but only that part in use for the day. The position of the markers is varied from day to day to avoid undue wear and tear of turf.

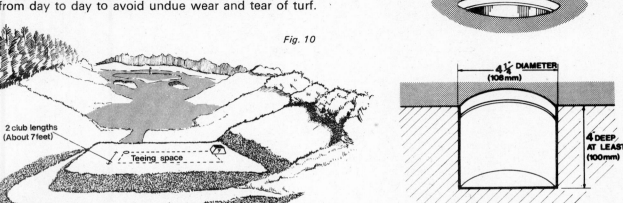

Fig. 11

Fig. 10

2 club lengths
(About 7 feet)

Teeing space

4¼ DIAMETER
(108 mm)

4 DEEP
AT LEAST
(100 mm)

Definition 15: The "hole" shall be 4¼ inches (108 mm) in diameter and at least 4 inches (100 mm) deep. If a lining be used it shall be sunk at least 1 inch (25 mm) below the putting green surface unless the nature of the soil makes it impractical to do so. Its outer diameter shall not exceed 4¼ inches.

Rule 13
PLAYING OUTSIDE TEEING GROUND
If a player in a match, when starting a hole, plays a ball from outside the teeing ground there is no penalty, but his opponent may require him to replay the stroke from within the teeing ground. In stroke play, however, he must replay the stroke from the proper place, counting the illegal stroke made. If a competitor fails to rectify his mistake before making a stroke off the next teeing ground or, in the case of the last hole of the round, before leaving the putting green, he shall be disqualified.

A player may take his stance outside the teeing ground to play a ball within it.

Rule 14

BALL FALLING OFF TEE

If a ball, when not in play (that is, when a stroke has not yet been made at it) falls off a tee, or is knocked off by the player, in addressing it, it may be re-teed without penalty.

Rule 15

ORDER OF PLAY IN THREESOME AND FOURSOME

In a foursome (two players playing one ball against a similar pair) the partners shall strike off alternately from the teeing grounds (*A* drives at the first hole and *B* at the second, etc.) and thereafter the partners shall strike alternately during the play of each hole. In match play if a player plays when his partner should have played, his side loses the hole. The penalty in stroke play is two strokes, or disqualification if the stroke is not rectified by replaying the stroke in the correct order.

Rule 16

BALL PLAYED AS IT LIES AND NOT TOUCHED

The ball shall be played as it lies and shall not be purposely moved or purposely touched except that the player may, without penalty, touch his ball with his club in the act of addressing it, and except as otherwise provided in the Rules or Local Rules.

Fig. 12

**Ball falls off tee
NO PENALTY**

Rule 17

IMPROVING LIE OR STANCE AND INFLUENCING BALL PROHIBITED

Irregularities of surface which could in any way affect a player's lie shall not be removed or pressed down by the player, his partner, or either of their caddies except (*a*) as may occur in fairly taking his stance, (*b*) in making the stroke, (*c*) when teeing a ball or (*d*) repairing damage to the putting green under Rule 35–1 (c).

If the ball lies in long grass, rushes, bushes, whins, heather or the like, only so much thereof shall be touched as will enable the player to find and identify his ball: nothing shall be done which can in any way improve its lie.

A player shall not improve, or allow to be improved, his line of play, the position or lie of his ball, or the area of his intended swing, by bending, moving or breaking anything fixed or growing (except in taking a fair stance to address the ball, and in making the stroke).

Rule 18

LOOSE IMPEDIMENTS

Any loose impediment may be removed without penalty except when both the impediment and the ball lie in or touch a hazard. When a ball is in motion a loose impediment shall not be removed.

The term "loose impediments" denotes natural objects not fixed or growing and not adhering to the

Legal

Improving lie or stance prohibited except on tee

Illegal

Fig. 13

Fig. 14

Illegal

ball, and includes stones not solidly embedded, leaves, twigs, branches and the like, dung, worms and insects and casts or heaps made by them.

Snow and ice are either casual water or loose impediments, at the option of the player.

Sand and loose soil are loose impediments on the putting green, but not elsewhere on the course.

Rule 19

STRIKING AT BALL

The ball shall be firmly struck at with the head of the club, and must not be pushed, scraped or spooned.

If the player, when making a stroke, strikes the ball twice he shall count the stroke and add a penalty stroke—making in all two.

Scoop

Fig. 15

Rule 20

BALL FARTHER FROM THE HOLE PLAYED FIRST

When the balls are "in play" the ball furthest from the hole shall be played first. In match play on the green or in a hazard if a player plays when his opponent should have done so the opponent may immediately require the player to replay the stroke.

Rule 21

PLAYING A WRONG BALL OR FROM A WRONG PLACE

A player must hole out with the ball driven from the teeing ground unless a Rule or Local Rule permits him to substitute another ball.

Note: Generally there is a penalty of two strokes in stroke play or loss of hole in match play for playing the wrong ball, but if a player in a stroke competition holes out with the wrong ball he is disqualified, unless he rectifies his mistake by finding and holing out with his own ball from the place where the mistake occurred. In match play if each side plays the other side's ball and it cannot be settled which side first committed the error, the hole shall be played out with the balls thus exchanged.

Rules 22 and 23

LIFTING, DROPPING, PLACING, IDENTIFYING OR CLEANING BALL

Through the green or in a hazard, when a ball is lifted under a Rule or Local Rule or when another ball is to be played, it shall be dropped as near as possible to the spot where the ball lay, except when a rule permits it to be dropped elsewhere or placed. In a hazard, a ball must be dropped and come to rest in the hazard; if it rolls out of the hazard it must be re-dropped without penalty. (If on a putting green the ball shall be placed.)

A ball shall be dropped by the player himself. He shall face the hole, stand erect, and drop the ball behind him over his shoulder. If a ball be dropped in any other manner the player shall incur a penalty stroke. If the ball touch the player before it strikes the ground, the player shall re-drop without penalty. If the ball touch the player after it strikes the ground the ball shall be played as it rests or if it comes to rest against the player and move when he then moves, there is no penalty.

A ball to be lifted under the rules should be lifted by the owner or his partner or by either of their caddies, or by another person authorised by the owner. It may be lifted for the purpose of identification but must then be replaced on the same spot in the presence of the player's opponent or marker. A ball may be cleaned when lifted from an unplayable lie, for relief from an obstruction, from casual water, or ground under repair, from a water hazard or on the putting green. Otherwise, during the play of a hole a player may not clean a ball, except to the extent necessary for identification or if permitted by Local Rules.

Note: For precise details of these rules, the Rules of Golf should be consulted.

Dropping a ball
Direction of play ⟶

Fig. 16

Rule 24

BALL INTERFERING WITH PLAY

Through the green or in a hazard, a player may have any other ball lifted if he considers that it might interfere

Fig. 17

Lifting a ball

with his play. A ball so lifted shall be replaced after the player has played his stroke. If a ball be accidentally moved when complying with this rule, no penalty shall be incurred, but the ball so moved shall be replaced.

Rule 25

A MOVING BALL

A player shall not play whilst his ball is moving, with the exception of certain cases, e.g., when the ball is moving in water.

Penalty

Fig. 18

Rule 26

BALL IN MOTION STOPPED OR DEFLECTED

If a ball in motion be stopped or deflected by any outside agency, it is a "rub of the green" and the ball shall be played as it lies, without penalty.

If it lodges in anything moving, a ball shall be dropped or placed as near as possible to the spot where the moving object was when the ball lodged in it, without penalty.

If the player's ball in motion be stopped or deflected by him, his partner or either of their caddies, or their clubs or other equipment, the player or his side shall lose two strokes in stroke play or lose the hole in match play. If it be stopped by anyone or anything on the opposing side in match play the opponent shall lose the hole.

Rule 27

BALL AT REST MOVED

If a ball at rest be moved or the lie altered by an opponent, a fellow-competitor or the caddie of either or any outside agency except wind, the player shall replace the ball, without penalty to himself. If it be impossible to determine the exact spot, the ball shall be dropped (or placed on the putting green) as near as possible to the place from which it was moved, and not nearer the hole.

Except while searching for the ball, if it is moved by the opponent (in match play) the opponent shall incur a penalty stroke, and the ball shall be replaced. If it is moved by the player whether while searching or not, he shall incur a penalty stroke, and the ball shall be played as it lies. In a stroke competition if the ball is moved by a fellow competitor or anyone on the fellow competitor's side, there is no penalty but the ball must be restored to its original position, but if the ball is moved by the player he shall incur a penalty stroke.

Ball accidentally moved
If by player, 1 stroke penalty
If by anyone else, no penalty

Outside agency

Fig. 19

Fig. 20

Rule 28

BALL UNFIT FOR PLAY

If a ball in play be so damaged as to be unfit for further play it may be changed by the player on his intimating to his opponent his intention of doing so. Mud on a ball does not make it unfit for play.

Out of bounds

Fig. 21

Rule 29

BALL LOST, OUT OF BOUNDS OR UNPLAYABLE

If a ball be lost outside a water hazard or be out of bounds, the player shall play his next stroke as nearly as possible at the spot from which the original ball was played or moved by him, adding a penalty stroke to his

Ball unplayable

Fig. 22

score for the hole. A ball may be declared unplayable at any place on the course except in a water hazard, and the player is the sole judge as to whether his ball is unplayable. If a player deems his ball to be unplayable he shall either (*a*) play his next stroke as provided for a ball lost or out of bounds, i.e. the "stroke and distance" penalty, or (*b*) drop a ball, under a penalty of one stroke, either within two club-lengths of the point where the ball lay, but not nearer the hole; or behind the point where the ball lay, keeping that point between himself and the hole, with no limit to how far behind that point the ball may be dropped. If the ball lay in a bunker, a ball must be dropped in the bunker.

Rule 30

PROVISIONAL BALL

If a ball may be lost outside a water hazard or may be out of bounds, to save time the player may at once play another ball provisionally as nearly as possible from the spot at which the original ball was played. Before playing a provisional ball the player must announce his intention to his opponent or marker, and such a ball may be played only before the player or his partner goes forward to search for the original ball. The player may play a provisional ball until he reaches the place where the original ball is likely to be. If he play any strokes with the provisional ball from the point beyond that place, the original ball is deemed to be lost. If the original ball be lost outside a water hazard or be out of bounds he shall continue play with the provisional ball under penalty of stroke and distance. If the original ball

be unplayable in bounds, or lie or be lost in a water hazard, the provisional ball shall be abandoned.

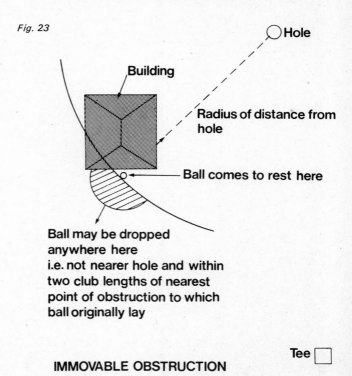

Fig. 23

Hole

Building

Radius of distance from hole

Ball comes to rest here

Ball may be dropped anywhere here i.e. not nearer hole and within two club lengths of nearest point of obstruction to which ball originally lay

Tee

IMMOVABLE OBSTRUCTION

Rule 31

OBSTRUCTIONS

Any movable obstruction (that is, anything artificially erected or placed on the course or left there temporarily) may be removed before a shot is played. If the obstruction is immovable, or the ball lies on it or touching it, the ball may be lifted and dropped or placed not more than two club-lengths away, without penalty, and must come to rest not nearer the hole. See Fig. 23.

Rule 32

CASUAL WATER

If a player's ball lies in or touches casual water, ground under repair or a hole, cast or runway made by a burrowing animal, a reptile or a bird, or if any of these conditions interfere with the player's stance or the area of his intended swing . . . he may drop a ball without penalty on ground which avoids these conditions, within two club-lengths of the margin of such area nearest to which the ball originally lay, but not nearer the hole. He may also drop a ball similarly in a hazard without penalty, but if a ball is dropped clear of the hazard there is a penalty stroke.

If a ball lies in casual water on the putting green, or if casual water intervenes between it and the hole, the ball may be lifted and placed, without penalty, on the nearest spot (not nearer the hole) which will give a clear line to the hole.

Fig. 24

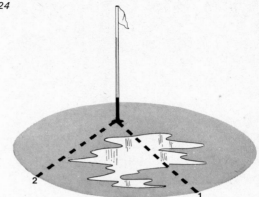

Casual water—ball may be moved from 1 to 2

Rule 33

HAZARDS AND WATER HAZARDS

When the ball lies in or touches a hazard or water hazard nothing shall be done which can in any way improve its lie. Before making a stroke, the player shall not touch the ground or water with his club, nor touch or move any loose impediment in the hazard.

If the ball lies or is lost in a water hazard, the player can play the ball as it lies, or, under a penalty of one stroke, drop a ball: (*a*) behind the water hazard, without limit as to distance, keeping the spot at which the ball last crossed the margin of the hazard between himself and the hole, or (*b*) as near as possible to the spot

Fig. 25

Water hazard

Lateral water hazard

Fig. 26

Touching ground prohibited

Fig. 27

28

from which the original ball was played.

A player may drop a ball outside a lateral water hazard within two club-lengths of the margin of either side, opposite the point where the ball last crossed the hazard margin. The ball must come to rest not nearer the hole.

Note: Hazards are of various kinds, but bunkers form by far the greatest number of such hazards on most golf courses. Bunkers are depressions in the ground filled with sand, and usually built up on the side nearest the hole, so that the player must loft the ball out, thus losing considerable distance in relation to an opponent lying on the fairway. Most bunkers, however, are around the greens, and considerable skill is required to get the ball out and near enough to the hole to have a chance of getting down in one putt. Lateral water hazards must be so defined by the Committee.

Scraping sand to see top of ball

Fig. 28

Rule 34

THE FLAGSTICK

The player may have the flagstick attended, removed or held up to indicate the position of the hole, at any time. This may be done only on the authority of the player before he plays his stroke. If the flagstick be attended or removed by an opponent, a fellow-competitor, or the caddie of either, with the knowledge of the player, and no objection is made, the player shall be deemed to have authorised it.

If a player's ball strikes the flagstick when it is attended or has been removed, or if it strikes the person standing at the flagstick or equipment carried by him, or if it strikes an unattended flagstick when played from the putting green, the player shall incur a penalty of loss of hole in match play or two strokes in stroke play.

If the ball rests against the flagstick when it is in the hole, the player shall be entitled to have the flagstick removed, and if the ball falls into the hole the player shall be deemed to have holed out at his last stroke.

Fig. 29

The flagstick

Rule 35

THE PUTTING GREEN

The line of the putt must not be touched except as provided in other parts of this rule, but the player may place the club in front of the ball when addressing it, without pressing anything down. The player may move any loose impediment on the putting green by picking it up or brushing it aside with his hand or a club, without pressing anything down. If the ball be moved, it shall be replaced, without penalty.

The player may repair damage to the putting green caused by the impact of a ball. The ball may be lifted to permit repair and shall be replaced on the spot from which it was lifted.

A ball lying on the putting green may be lifted and cleaned without penalty and replaced on the spot from which it was lifted; in match play the ball must be replaced immediately if the opponent so requests.

When the ball nearer the hole lies on the putting green, if the player considers it might interfere with his play, he may require the opponent to lift the ball, which must be replaced after the player has played his stroke.

Anyone on the player's side may, before a stroke is made, point out a line for putting, but the following are prohibited:

Placing a mark on the green; touching line of putt in front of, to the side of, or behind the hole; testing surface of green or rolling a ball on it or roughening or scraping the surface; playing before the other ball is at rest; standing so as to influence position or movement of ball; lifting other ball while player's ball is in motion.

A ball lying on a putting green other than that of the hole being played must be lifted and dropped off the putting green, not nearer the hole, without penalty, as near as possible to where the ball lay.

The player shall not make a stroke on the putting green from a stance astride, or with either foot touching the line of the putt or an extension of the line behind the ball.

Match Play. Putting out of turn: the opponent may require the stroke to be replayed, in match play.

Player's ball knocking opponent's ball into the hole: the opponent is deemed to have holed out at his last stroke. A ball moved by the other ball may be replaced.

In match play a player after holing out may remove the opponent's ball, provided it is at rest, claiming the hole or conceding the half as the case may be. If the opponent's ball is not removed and it falls into the hole, the opponent is deemed to have holed out at his last stroke.

Flagstick being held to indicate position of hole

Fig. 30

Fig 31

Fig. 32

Loose impediments

Pitch marks may be repaired

Stroke Play. In stroke play if the ball nearer the hole is in the way or affecting the playing of the other ball in any way, it may be played first or lifted while the other ball is played, but only at the request of the player about to putt.

In stroke play the ball may be lifted or putted first if the owner considers it might be of assistance to a fellow competitor.

When both balls lie on the putting green, if the competitor's ball strikes the other he shall incur a penalty of two strokes and play his ball as it lies. The other ball shall be at once replaced.

Fig. 33

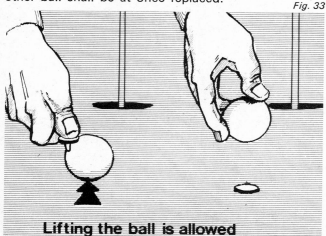

Lifting the ball is allowed

Fig. 34

Prohibited: Touching line of putt in front of, to side of, or behind the hole

PUTTING

Putting is the most precise part of the game and the most important, for strokes can be saved by good putting and wasted by bad putting. The normal average allowance is two putts per green, but any golfer who is doing well usually beats this average.

When the ball lies a fair distance from the hole the stroke is called an "approach putt", and demands accurate judgement of strength and line. If the green at that part is level, it may be a "straight putt", but more often the stroke requires a "borrow" (the ball is then aimed at a point to right or left to allow for the slope).

Then the player must estimate the strength of the putt. If the green slopes down towards the hole, less power will be required than if the putt is uphill. Again, the green might be "slow" after rain or because the grass has grown, or "fast" because of hot sunshine or strong wind. This is the one area of the game where the Vardon grip is not used and is replaced by a grip with the thumb directly down the handle.

Having summed up the situation to his own satisfaction, the player makes a trial swing to make sure he has the desired stroke well in mind, and then gets his putter blade at right-angles to the intended line and immediately behind the ball. He takes a short or long back-swing, according to the type of stroke, and delivers a firm, smooth stroke, keeping the putter blade as far as possible on the line intended.

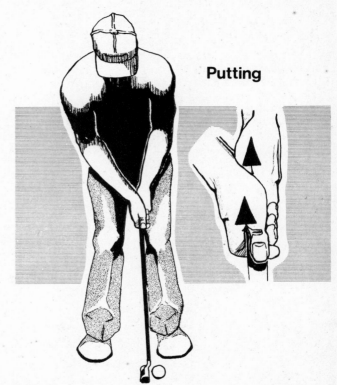

Putting

Fig. 35

KEEPING THE SCORE

Cards like the specimen shown are used for marking a competitor's score in a Medal, Stableford or Match Play Against Par competition. In Medal play the competitor's full handicap is deducted from his total score. In Stableford competitions seven-eighths of the handicap is taken and in Match Play Against Par competitions three-quarters of the handicap is taken. In matches the player with the higher handicap receives three-quarters of the difference between him and his opponent.

Column 1 gives No. of hole.

Column 2 gives length of hole, measured from competition tees.

Column 3 gives the par of the hole.

Column 4 indicates where handicap strokes are taken in Match Play Against Par or Stableford competitions. For example, a player having 12 strokes takes one at the 5th (numbered 12) and one each at all other holes having figures less than 12. A player having only three strokes takes them at the 2nd, 9th and 14th holes.

Column 5 is for the player's score in strokes. This is always given as the gross score, the number of strokes actually played and inserted by marker. Handicap calculations are made afterwards.

LOCKHEATH GOLF CLUB
STANDARD SCRATCH SCORE 70
Date 1/1/75
Handicap 16 *

Player J. SNOOKS * Competition Match play against par * Strokes Received 12 *

Hole	Yards	Par	Stroke Index	Players Score	Won X Lost — Halved O	Hole	Yards	Par	Stroke Index	Players Score	Won X Lost — Halved O
1	460	4	14	7	—*	10	350	4	- 11	6	—*
2	390	4	- 3	4	+*	11	350	4	- 6	4	+*
3	430	4	16	6	—*	12	165	3	15	3	O*
4	195	3	- 7	3	+*	13	510	5	-10	6	O*
5	335	4	-12	5	O*	14	360	4	- 2	5	O*
6	480	5	- 5	6	O*	15	345	4	- 8	4	+*
7	350	4	- 9	4	+*	16	140	3	17	4	—*
8	115	3	18	6	—*	17	400	4	- 4	5	O*
9	360	4	- 1	5	O*	18	295	4	13	4	O*
OUT	3115	35		46	*	IN	2915	35		41	*

Markers Signature M. Smith
Competitors Signature J. Snooks

Match play against par
Holes Won 5
Holes Lost 5
Holes Halved 8
Result ALL SQUARE

OUT	3115	35	46	*
	6030	70	87	*
HANDICAP			16	*
NET SCORE			71	*

Fig. 36

Column 6 shows the result of each hole compared with par. If the player's net score for the hole (after deducting any handicap stroke) is less than the par score he marks a + indicating a win. If the score is the same the Committee marks a 0, indicating a halved hole. If the score is higher the Committee marks a — indicating a loss.

The card shown at left is marked out for a player having gone round in 71 net, and finishing one over par in a stroke play competition, or finishing all square in a Match Play Against Par competition. The stars indicate those items which are the Committee's responsibility. Both the player and marker *must* sign the card before it is handed in.

Readers are strongly advised to read the Rules of Golf in full, but for their information Sections I and II, concerning Etiquette and Definitions, are reproduced here.

ETIQUETTE

Courtesy On The Course

CONSIDERATION FOR OTHER PLAYERS

In the interest of all, players should play without delay.

No player should play until the players in front are out of range.

Players searching for a ball should signal the players behind them to pass as soon as it becomes apparent that the ball will not easily be found; they should not search for five minutes before doing so. They should not continue play until the players following them have passed and are out of range.

When the play of a hole has been completed, players should immediately leave the putting green.

BEHAVIOUR DURING PLAY

No one should move, talk or stand close to or directly behind the ball or the hole when a player is addressing the ball or making a stroke.

The player who has the honour should be allowed to play before his opponent or fellow-competitor tees his ball.

Priority On The Course

In the absence of special rules, two-ball matches should have precedence of and be entitled to pass any three- or four-ball matches.

A single player has no standing and should give way to a match of any kind.

Any match playing a whole round is entitled to pass a match playing a shorter round.

If a match fails to keep its place on the course and loses more than one clear hole on the players in front, it should allow the match following to pass.

Care Of The Course

HOLES IN BUNKERS

Before leaving a bunker, a player should carefully fill up and smooth over all holes and footprints made by him.

RESTORE DIVOTS AND BALL-MARKS

Through the green, a player should ensure that any turf cut or displaced by him is replaced at once and pressed down, and that any damage to the putting green made by the ball or the player is carefully repaired.

DAMAGE TO GREENS—FLAGSTICKS, BAGS, ETC.

Players should ensure that, when putting down bags, or the flagstick, no damage is done to the putting green, and that neither they nor their caddies damage the hole by standing close to it, in handling the flagstick or in removing the ball from the hole. The flagstick should be properly replaced in the hole before the players leave the putting green.

GOLF CARTS

Local Notices regulating the movement of golf carts should be strictly observed.

DAMAGE THROUGH PRACTICE SWINGS

In taking practice swings players should avoid causing damage to the course, particularly to tees, by removing divots.

DEFINITIONS

1 ADDRESSING THE BALL

A player has "addressed the ball" when he has taken his stance and has also grounded his club, except that in a hazard a player has addressed the ball when he has taken his stance.

2. ADVICE

"Advice" is any counsel or suggestion which could influence a player in determining his play, the choice of a club, or the method of making a stroke.

Information on the Rules or Local Rules is not advice.

3. BALL DEEMED TO MOVE

A ball is deemed to have "moved" if it leaves its position and comes to rest in any other place.

4. BALL HOLED

A ball is "holed" when it lies within the circumference of the hole and all of it is below the level of the lip of the hole.

5. BALL IN PLAY, PROVISIONAL BALL, WRONG BALL

a. A ball is "in play" as soon as the player has made a stroke on the teeing ground. It remains as his ball in play until holed out, except when it is out of bounds, lost or lifted, or another ball has been substituted under an applicable Rule or Local Rule: a ball so substituted becomes the ball in play.

b. A "provisional ball" is a ball played under Rule 30 for a ball which may be lost outside a water hazard or may be out of bounds. It ceases to be a provisional ball when the Rule provides either that the player continues play with it as the ball in play or that it be abandoned.

c. A "wrong ball" is any ball other than the ball in play or a provisional ball or, in stroke play, an alternate ball played in accordance with Rule 11–5.

6. BALL LOST

A ball is "lost" if:

a. It be not found, or be not identified as his by the player, within five minutes after the player's side or his or their caddies have begun to search for it; or

b. The player has put another ball into play under the Rules, even though he may not have searched for the original ball; or

c. The player, having played a provisional ball under Rule 30–1, either

(i) abandons his original ball as lost (Rule 29–3), even though he may not have searched for it, or

(ii) plays any stroke with the provisional ball from a point beyond the place where the original ball is likely to be, whereupon the provisional ball becomes the ball in play.

Play of a provisional ball under Rule 30 or of a wrong ball does not constitute abandonment of the ball in play. Time spent in playing a wrong ball is not counted in the five-minute period allowed for search.

7. CADDIE, FORECADDIE AND EQUIPMENT

a. A "caddie" is one who carries or handles a player's clubs during play and otherwise assists him in accordance with the Rules.

When one caddie is employed by more than one player, he is always deemed to be the caddie of the player whose ball is involved, and equipment carried by him is deemed to be that player's equipment, except when the caddie acts upon specific directions of another player, in which case he is considered to be that other player's caddie.

Note: In threesome, foursome, best-ball and four-ball play, a caddie carrying for more than one player should be assigned to the members of one side.

b. A "forecaddie" is one employed by the Committee to indicate to players the position of balls on the course, and is an outside agency (Definition 22).

c. "Equipment" is anything used, worn or carried by or for the player except his ball in play. Equipment includes a golf cart. If such cart is shared by more than one player, its status under the Rules is the same as that of a caddie employed by more than one player.

8. CASUAL WATER

"Casual water" is any temporary accumulation of water which is visible before or after the player takes his stance and which is not a hazard of itself or is not a water hazard. Snow and ice are either casual water or loose impediments, at the option of the player.

9. COMMITTEE

The "Committee" is the committee in charge of the competition.

10. COMPETITOR

A "competitor" is a player in a stroke competition. A "fellow-competitor" is any person with whom the competitor plays. Neither is partner of the other. In stroke play foursome and four-ball competitions, where the context so admits, the word "competitor" or "fellow-competitor" shall be held to include his partner.

11. COURSE

The "course" is the whole area within which play is permitted. It is the duty of the Committee to define its boundaries accurately.

12. FLAGSTICK

The "flagstick" is a movable straight indicator provided by the Committee, with or without bunting or other material attached, centred in the hole to show its position. It shall be circular in cross-section.

13. GROUND UNDER REPAIR

"Ground under repair" is any portion of the course so marked by order of the committee concerned or so declared by its authorised representative. It includes material piled for removal and a hole made by a greenkeeper, even if not so marked. Stakes and lines defining ground under repair are not in such ground.

14. HAZARDS

A "hazard" is any bunker or water hazard. Bare patches, scrapes, roads, tracks and paths are not hazards.

a. A "bunker" is an area of bare ground, often a depression which is usually covered with sand. Grass-covered ground bordering or within a bunker is not part of the hazard.

b. A "water hazard" is any sea, lake, pond, river, ditch, surface drainage ditch or other open water course (regardless of whether or not it contains water), and anything of a similar nature.

All ground or water within the margin of a water hazard, whether or not it be covered with any growing substance, is part of the water hazard. The margin of a water hazard is deemed to extend vertically upwards.

c. A "lateral water hazard" is a water hazard or that part of a water hazard running approximately parallel to the line of play and so situated that it is not possible to drop the ball behind the water hazard and keep the spot at which the ball last crossed the hazard margin between the player and the hole. The Committee may declare any water hazard or any part of a water hazard to be a lateral water hazard.

d. It is the duty of the Committee in charge of a course to define accurately the extent of the hazards and water hazards when there is any doubt. That part of a hazard to be played as a lateral water hazard should be distinctively marked. Stakes and lines defining margins of hazards are not in the hazards.

15. HOLE

The "hole" shall be $4\frac{1}{4}$ inches (108 mm) in diameter and at least 4 inches (100 mm) deep. If a lining be used, it shall be sunk at least 1 inch (25 mm) below the putting green surface unless the nature of the soil makes it impractical to do so; its outer diameter shall not exceed $4\frac{1}{4}$ inches (108 mm).

16. HONOUR

The side which is entitled to play first from the teeing ground is said to have the "honour".

17. LOOSE IMPEDIMENTS

The term "loose impediments" denotes natural objects not fixed or growing and not adhering to the ball, and includes stones not solidly embedded, leaves, twigs, branches, and the like, dung, worms and insects and casts or heaps made by them. Snow and ice are either casual water or loose impediments, at the option of the player.

Sand and loose soil are loose impediments on the putting green, but not elsewhere on the course.

18. MARKER

A "marker" is a scorer in stroke play who is appointed by the Committee to record a competitor's score. He may be a fellow-competitor. He is not a referee. A marker should not lift a ball or mark its position unless authorised to do so by the competitor and,

unless he is a fellow-competitor, should not attend the flagstick or stand at the hole or mark its position.

19. OBSERVER

An "observer' is appointed by the Committee to assist a referee to decide questions of fact and to report to him any breach of a Rule or Local Rule. An observer should not attend the flagstick, stand at or mark the position of the hole, or lift the ball or mark its position.

20. OBSTRUCTIONS

An "obstruction" is anything artificial, whether erected, placed or left on the course, except:

a. Objects defining out of bounds, such as walls, fences, stakes and railings;

b. Artificial surfaces and sides of roads and paths;

c. In water hazards, artificially surfaced banks or beds, including bridge supports when part of such a bank. Bridges and bridge supports which are not part of such a bank are obstructions;

d. Any construction declared by the Committee to be an integral part of the course.

21. OUT OF BOUNDS

"Out of bounds" is ground on which play is prohibited.

When out of bounds is fixed by stakes or a fence, the out of bounds line is determined by the nearest inside points of the stakes or fence posts at ground level: the line is deemed to extend vertically upwards. When out of bounds is fixed by a line on the grounds the line itself is out of bounds.

A ball is out of bounds when all of it lies out of bounds.

22. OUTSIDE AGENCY

An "outside agency" is any agency not part of the match or, in stroke play, not part of a competitor's side, and includes a referee, a marker, an observer, or a forecaddie employed by the Committee.

23. PARTNER

A "partner" is a player associated with another player on the same side. In a threesome, foursome or a four-ball where the context so admits, the word "player" shall be held to include his partner.

24. PENALTY STROKE
A "penalty stroke" is one added to the score of a side under certain Rules. It does not affect the order of play.

25. PUTTING GREEN
The "putting green" is all ground of the hole being played which is specially prepared for putting or otherwise defined as such by the Committee.

A ball is deemed to be on the putting green when any part of it touches the putting green.

26. REFEREE
A "referee" is a person who has been appointed by the Committee to accompany players to decide questions of fact and of golf law. He shall act on any breach of Rule or Local Rule which he may observe or which may be reported to him by an observer (see Definition 19).

In stroke play the Committee may limit a referee's duties.

A referee should not attend the flagstick, stand at or mark the position of the hole or lift the ball or mark its position.

27. RUB OF THE GREEN
A "rub of the green" occurs when a ball in motion is stopped or deflected by any outside agency.

28. SIDES AND MATCHES
Side	A player or two or more players who are partners.
Single	A match in which one plays against another.
Threesome	A match in which one plays against two, and each side plays one ball.
Foursome	A match in which two play against two, and each side plays one ball.
Three-ball	A match in which three play against one another, each playing his own ball.
Best-ball	A match in which one plays against the better ball of two or the best ball of three players.
Four-ball	A match in which two play their better ball against the better ball of two other players.

Note: In a best-ball or four-ball match, if a partner be absent for reasons satisfactory to the Committee, the remaining member(s) of his side may represent the side.

29. STANCE
Taking the "stance" consists in a player placing his feet in position for and preparatory to making a stroke.

30. STIPULATED ROUND
The "stipulated round" consists of playing the holes of the course in their correct sequence unless otherwise authorised by the Committee. The number of holes in a stipulated round is 18 unless a smaller number is authorised by the Committee.

In match play only, the Committee may, for the purpose of settling a tie, extend the stipulated round to as many holes as are required for a match to be won.

31. STROKE
A "stroke" is the forward movement of the club made with the intention of fairly striking at and moving the ball.

32. TEEING
In "teeing", the ball may be placed on the ground or on sand or other substance in order to raise it off the ground.

33. TEEING GROUND
The "teeing ground" is the starting place for the hole to be played. It is a rectangular area two club-lengths in depth, the front and the sides of which are defined by the outside limits of two markers. A ball is outside the teeing ground when all of it lies outside the stipulated area.

34. TERMS USED IN RECKONING IN MATCH PLAY
In match play, the reckoning of holes is kept by the terms: so many "holes up" or "all square" and so many "to play".

A side is "dormie" when it is as many holes up as there are holes remaining to be played.

35. THROUGH THE GREEN
"Through the green" is the whole area of the course except:
a. Teeing ground and putting green of the hole being played;
b. All hazards on the course.

KTG KNOW THE GAME

Every major sport and pastime is covered in this well-known, best-selling series, with over 70 titles. Each is fully illustrated with clear, concise explanations of the rules and the basic principles of the activity concerned. Prepared with the official Association, and regularly revised to incorporate rule changes.

Each book measures $5\frac{1}{4}$" x 8", and costs 35p to 40p.

TITLES IN THE SERIES INCLUDE:-

Archery, Association Football, Athletics, Backgammon, Badminton, Basketball, Billiards and Snooker, Bowls, Camping, Caravanning, Card Games, Care of Your Pets, Chess, Coarse Fishing, Contract Bridge, Cricket, Croquet, Crossword Solving, Cycling, Cycle Racing, Dancing, Fencing, Folk Dancing, Golf, Gymnastics, Inn Games, Judo, Karate, Kayak Canoeing, Keeping Fit, Lacrosse, Lawn Tennis, Life Saving, Map Reading, Men's Hockey, Motor Boating and Water Skiing, Motor Cycling, Motor Sport, Netball, Orienteering, Photography, Pigeon Racing, Potholing and Caving, Rambling and Youth Hostelling, Riding, Rock Climbing, Roller Skating, Rounders, Rowing, Rugby League Football, Rugby Union Football, Sailing, Schoolboy Boxing, Scrabble, Sea Angling, Shot Gun Shooting, Show Jumping, Skiing, Squash Rackets, Stamp Collecting, Swimming, Swimming to Win, Table Tennis, Target Shooting, Tenpin Bowling, Trampolining, Underwater Swimming, Volleyball, Water Polo, Weight Lifting, Women's Hockey, Wrestling, Yoga.

Obtainable from your local bookshop and bookseller or

 **EP PUBLISHING LIMITED**
Bradford Road, East Ardsley, Wakefield, West Yorkshire